Saying YES To You

WHAT THE BIBLE SAYS ABOUT SELF-CARE

DAILY DEVOTIONAL

by

PAMELA ZIMMER

Cover design: Fiverr
Author photo: Taylor Boone Photography

Printed in the United States of America

ISBN: 0991294335
ISBN-13: 978-0991294336

DEDICATION

This book is dedicated to all the people who have believed in me, trusted me, walked with me, encouraged me, carried me, lifted me and who see me. You are the ones I show up for. You are the ones I work to be a better person for. You are the ones who I can stand in front of and humbly say,

"All Glory to God."

PAMELA ZIMMER

CONTENTS

PAMELA ZIMMER

ACKNOWLEDGEMENTS

"None of us got to where we are alone. Whether the assistance we received was obvious or subtle, acknowledging someone's help is a big part of understanding the importance of saying thank you."
-Harvey Mackay

I have several people to thank and give acknowledgement to today, so let me start here…

I would like to thank three specific women in my life who helped shape my walk with Jesus. Without them, I would not be on this walk with him, and who knows where my life would be.

These women, who do not generally know each other, know me. Individually they showed me what it was to be a Christian. Not by telling me, but by being an example themselves. They never shoved their faith down my throat or threw it in my face. They simply loved me. They lived their lives, invited me in, and slowly I began to get curious as to what made them "different."

To be honest, at first I was a little uncomfortable. They were happy and kind and loving - all the time! Did they ever have a bad day? I know now that they each are no different nor better than me, and we all have our share of bad days, but the way they each relied on their faith to get through, and continued to love no matter what - it was refreshing. It was new. It was something I wanted to know more about.

Dawn Heins, you were the first person I ever had the privilege of hearing God's word from. You opened your home to me every week and graced me with warm smiles, hot coffee and a deep-rooted love for the Bible. You were the first person I called when I was ready to buy my own Bible, and you shared in my excitement. You have taught me so much, I cannot even begin to express the breadth, and length, and depth, and height of my gratitude.

Stacey Palmer, I don't even know where to begin. I met you in the infancy of my faith. You answered my questions and shared your prayers with me. You prayed *for* me, without ever having to know the dark details. You showed me what it meant to pray hard, in circles. You were there for the biggest moment in my life, when I gave my life to Christ and was washed clean of all my sins, made new in the water. I am on this walk with you. Though our paths may take slightly different turns every so often, they always cross at just the right time, both leading to the same place. Thank you for being the light at my feet.

Marie Jackson, you kept your eyes on me, like the shepherd on his sheep. You bugged me, every single time you saw me, "Do you want to join MOPS?" You must have asked me a thousand times, but never with pressure or urgency. You knew something I didn't (yet), and boy am I glad I finally went to that very first meeting. You opened my world to grace and forgiveness. You let me cry with you, and then turn around and celebrate with you. You have trusted me with your heart, just as I know you so delicately hold mine as well. You continue to inspire me to be more bold in my faith, because I see you boldly in yours.

I want to next thank this woman for being the one who has showed me it's okay to show the mess. Life isn't perfect, even as a Christian - especially as a Christian! - and you continue to meet me right where I'm at. You're at my door when I need you, or on the other end of a late night text praying for me and my family. You have showed me how God uses us and grows us. I have watched you grow in your calling and it has allowed me to more fully step into mine. Crystal Reilley, thank you.

To Erin Oksol and Ly Piper Smith, you are my growth friends. How else does one write a book in seven days? You were the ones who encouraged me, got excited for me, felt inspired by me, and never, never judged me for what I was trying to do in such short time. It was never a question for either of you if I could do it, it was merely a question of what next? And now look, a two-year dream in living color. Everybody needs growth friends.

Lastly, but certainly not least, to my family. Will, you watched me as I sat at my computer this week, asking how it was going, not totally sure of exactly what I was writing, but allowing me the space to do it. You consistently get up with the boys in the morning and help put them to bed at night. You respect when my office door is closed, the classical music piping through my headphones, and my need for a little extra caffeine some mornings. I love you. I couldn't do any of what I do without you.

To my boys, the tears well every time I write to you. Amongst all the frustrations and repetition of being your mother, the joy and laughter and love you show me overshadows it all. Brayden, your goofy expression of life and your unapologetic expression of your love for Jesus takes my heart on the greatest roller coaster ride imaginable. Zackery, your passion and interest in what I'm doing (writing, speaking, teaching - whatever it is) has garnered you the title of my biggest fan. You both are my everything, and to say "I love you" is such a vast understatement.

To you all, I am grateful. Overflowing. My life is what it is because of you. My life is wonderful. How wonderful that we all get to watch each other in this wonderful life, on this wonderful walk with God.

"I thank you God for this most amazing day, for the leaping greenly spirits of trees, and for the blue dream of sky and for everything which is natural, which is infinite, which is yes."
-e. e. cummings

PREFACE

for it is God who works in you, both to will and to work for his good pleasure.
-Philippians 2:13 ESV

As I sat down to write this, originally I had planned for it to be only a seven-day devotional. Maybe I would stretch it out to ten days, but never was I thinking of doing an entire month. That was just not something I was qualified or ready to do.

We all know that God doesn't care if we think we're qualified. Well, I guess I shouldn't assume what you know. I know that God never needs my opinion on whether or not I feel qualified. The last five years of my life have been a clear example of this.

Two years ago I had the idea, the thought, "I want to write a devotional." I was doing one of my daily bible reading plans on my phone through the YouVersion® app. It's been part of my morning routine for quite some time and the more plans I do, the more I read and the more plans I want to do. It's a great addiction!

I thought if I could find seven, or maybe ten, verses of scripture to support my idea then surely I could write seven, or maybe ten, little blurbs of personal stories or teachings to go along with each verse. It couldn't be that hard, right?

For two years I sat on that idea. Thinking about it constantly, especially as I worked through bible reading plans that were ones I could have written - they were talking right to me! Have you ever read something and you had to look over your shoulder because you were certain the author was standing right there?

Fast forward to about ten days ago. I had just confirmed a dream speaking gig at my church. My presentation was going to be on how to get through the holiday hustle, keep our eyes on God, and what the Bible says about self-care. Hmm... interesting. The spark was lit.

Two days later I was meeting a new friend for coffee and what topic would you believe the conversation started and ended with? Devotionals. Throughout the rest of that day I kept getting hints and clues that maybe this was the right time, finally, to write my own devotional. God was speaking to me, telling me to write. He's done that before, but never quite like this.

So I thought, what if I could write a little seven, or maybe ten-day, devotional and have it ready for my presentations? It was a crazy idea. The timeline was tight. I'd have to be dedicated, and I couldn't waste any time adding all kinds of cute embellishments and different fonts. But I could do it, I really could do it. After all, God was telling me to "Go!"

The very next day I found myself back at that same coffee shop, this time with my Bible, my laptop and my headphones piping in classical music. Three and a half hours later I had researched all the verses I could find relating to my topic, without beating every single variation to death. Low and behold, I wound up having exactly thirty-one verses.

Okay God, I'm listening...

Seven days later, this thirty-one day devotional is complete.

God told me to write, so I wrote. Every word came so easily, as if it were from God - as I have no doubt it was. I am in awe of what He has done through me this week. And I am in even more awe that you are sitting here reading this. A real, live human being reading something that two years ago was just a thought and now one week later is real.

This month-long devotional isn't typical. Yes, you will still find a daily scripture, a little personal blurb from me, and space for reflection and prayer, but there aren't four weekly themes or equally divided sections.

Throughout this daily devotional you will find several themes. Some will take you through several days, while others you might only find yourself in for one or two days. Some days will have just one short verse, while others might be longer passages and/or a longer blurb. Trust that each day is what it is.

There is no theme that is more or less significant or important for you to grasp. They are all equally of value, treat them as such.

This has been designed specifically for you, with much thought and care. Things don't always look the way we want or expect them to. Beauty is often found between the cracks, amongst the weeds, or in the dirt underneath a stone. Do not miss out on the message because it looks different. Trust that you will find exactly what you are looking for each and every day - whether you are searching for it or not.

Find yourself a quiet spot, a warm cup of tea or coffee (or perhaps an iced cold glass of lemonade on a hot summer afternoon), and cozy up with God for the next thirty-one days. I can't wait to see what awesome things He does in your life!

INTRODUCTION

"An empty lantern provides no light. Self-care is the fuel that allows your light to shine brightly."
-Unknown

Do you ever feel like if you just had a few more hours or an extra day you could finish up whatever it is that you're working so hard on? Maybe it's a project at work, perhaps organizing a space in your home, or meal-planning and prep for the week ahead. Whatever it is, I'm sure - if you're anything like me - you just need a little more time to get it done.

Sometimes, we have no choice because there are deadlines out of our control (renewing your driver's license, for example... when it expires, it expires). But what about those times when we have full control of a perceived deadline? Have you ever stopped to think what would happen if you actually stopped for a little while? What would happen if you left the office at 5 o'clock? What would happen if you took a break from organizing that nice new bookcase? What would happen if your refrigerator wasn't perfectly color coded with pre-chopped bell peppers?

Sure, you might benefit from being able to quickly grab a healthy snack while running out the door (I'm certainly not discouraging that - and in fact, I could personally do a better job at it myself). The point is this: how much time are we spending just pushing through to get it done while sacrificing or missing out on quality time and rest?

I'll ask the question again. What would happen if you actually stopped?

I've recently been engaging in multiple conversations and discussions about how busy we are as a society. It's as if we walk around with this busy badge of honor saying "Hey, look at me! I'm so busy!" The busier we are, the more productive we feel. Productivity, however, has nothing to do with how busy we are. In fact, I argue to say that busyness is the exact and extreme opposite of productivity. They are on two different sides of the scale.

Oftentimes, we equate how busy we are with how successful we are. This is all wrong. Success has absolutely nothing to do with how busy we are. No amount of running around crazy, burning the midnight oil or owning the world's longest to-do list will ever get us to the top. And if you're one of the few for whom it actually does work out that way, I guarantee you can't sustain yourself at the rate you're going.

We also tend to equate how busy we are with our worth. "I must be important because I'm so busy." Have you ever thought that? Be honest... I have. Nothing and nobody gets to define our worth except for God. He created us in His image and we are worth far more than we give ourselves credit for. God defines who we are, not our ridiculous schedule.

We are stuck in this crazy fast-paced world, worried that if we stop for even just a moment we'll miss something. Or worse, we're worried that if we stop (*fill in the blank for whatever it is that you are constantly doing*), we won't know who we are.

We're complacent in letting our lives be defined by what we do. Our identity is tied so tightly around our work (a job or career, raising a family, or whatever you "do" day in and day out).

I'm here to say that our identity is not wrapped up in what we do. Our identity is *who we are*, not *what we do*.

We fear what we might be faced with if we stop. The question "Who am I?" begs to be answered. Yet only in the moments of stillness when we stop to give time to God can we. It is through eliminating the doing that currently consumes us, that we can even start to dissect that question. It's a question many of us fear the answer to, so it's easier to just ignore it and keep ourselves busy. But God wants us to know. He wants us to answer it. He wants us to be still with Him. God wants to show us who we really are. God wants us to know our identity. Our identity in Christ.

So, let me ask you one more time. What would happen if you *actually* stopped?

Think about it. Really think about it.

Life doesn't stop. The world keeps revolving. We have to have the knowledge, faith and courage to step off the merry-go-round every now and then. Otherwise we're just going to end up dizzy, hanging on for our dear life, forgetting why we're on this crazy ride to begin with. We don't want that!

It's okay to stop doing. It's okay to pause. It's okay to take a break. It's okay to rest. In fact, it's highly recommended and encouraged.

Science has researched and proven the benefits of rest. Benefits include greater focus and productivity, less sickness and lowered risk of illness, more engagement in relationships, higher levels of perceived happiness and joy, and greater feelings of connectedness to God and spirit.

Sounds pretty good to me! I'll take an order of that for here please, and pack one up in a doggy bag to go too.

In all seriousness, the reason I'm writing this is to show you how just a little bit of slowing down, taking a break and enjoying times of rest can benefit your entire life in ways you might not even imagine. By leading you to scripture and offering opportunities for reflection and prayer, my hope is that you will start to see a change in your life. A little more peace. An easier breath. A smile at night when your head hits the pillow.

Will you take this journey with me?

31 DAYS OF SAYING YES TO YOU

When you say "yes" to yourself you are allowing your best version to shine through. When you say "yes" to yourself you are showing others that you are valuable and see yourself through Christ's eyes - in His identity.
When you say "yes" to yourself you are inviting God to grow and shape you into the person He designed you to be.

Saying "yes" to you is a form of self-care. One might say it is the ultimate form of self-care because it demonstrates love for yourself on every single level, so that you may give love to others more freely, without depleting yourself to do it.

God commands us to love our neighbors as we love ourselves. We cannot love our neighbors unless we first know what it truly means to love ourselves - not in a selfish way, but in the way I will demonstrate to you that God intended - through self-care.

Leave your fear, your guilt and your tendencies to be a martyr at the door.

Come inside and day by day you will learn what the Bible says about self-care.

PAMELA ZIMMER

*"Learn to say 'no' to the good so you can say
'yes' to the best."*
-John C. Maxwell

*"Aim at heaven and you will get earth thrown in.
Aim at earth and you get neither."*
-C. S. Lewis

THE SABBATH

Day 1

1 Thus the heavens and the earth were finished, and all the host of them. 2 And on the seventh day God finished his work that he had done, and he rested on the seventh day from all his work that he had done. 3 So God blessed the seventh day and made it holy, because on it God rested from all his work that he had done in creation.

(Genesis 2:1-3 ESV)

In all of God's might and glory perhaps the greatest of all His creations was what He created on the seventh day... *nothing.*

Throughout the first six days He created the land and sea, the heavenly sky, the sun, the moon and all the stars that delicately hang in His precise placement. He created every creature, every plant, every form of living. On the seventh day He saw that what He created was good, very very good, and I can imagine the smile He showered down over everything. On this seventh day, God declared that nothing more needed to be done. Creation was complete. And so, He rested.

We are intentionally starting this daily devotional with the theme of Sabbath because of the foundation upon which everything else can build. Think about it, God created this day of rest on day seven.... how many days into life are we now? I think it's pretty significant that having a day of rest goes back that far. To the beginning.

REFLECTION & PRAYER:

_____

_____

_____

_____

_____

_____

_____

_____

_____

_____

_____

_____

_____

_____

_____

_____

Day 2

3 *Six days shall work be done, but on the seventh day is a Sabbath of solemn rest, a holy convocation. You shall do no work. It is a Sabbath to the Lord in all your dwelling places.*

(Leviticus 23:3 ESV)

We've all heard the saying "work hard, play hard." God was the ultimate - and first - example of this logic. But I don't think He meant it to be entirely what we have come to interpret it as today. This "work hard, play hard" mentality implies a level of hustle and busyness that is necessary, and unfortunately even expected in today's society. The only way to counterbalance this over-working it is to have equal periods of play time. It also suggests that play (or rest) is only deserved and warranted after hard periods of work.

Work ethic is not in question here. What's in question is the assumption that playing hard without working hard first is not generally accepted.

I think we can all agree that God did some pretty hefty work during those first six days. Again, that's not what is in question here. I don't believe that the only reason God rested on the seventh day was because He worked super hard the six days prior.

I believe God created and declared the seventh day a day of rest because in all His omnipotence, He knew how important rest was, and is.

REFLECTION & PRAYER:

_____

_____

_____

_____

_____

_____

_____

_____

_____

_____

_____

_____

_____

_____

_____

_____

_____

_____

_____

_____

_____

_____

_____

_____

_____

_____

_____

Day 3

27 And he said to them, **The Sabbath was made for man, not man for the Sabbath.**

(Mark 2:27 ESV)

To be honest, I actually had to look up a deeper meaning of this verse. It helps to share a little of the back story. You can look it up for yourself in Mark 2:23-28, but here's the gist of it. Jesus and his disciples were walking in a field on a Sabbath day, and they began to pluck some heads of grain. The Pharisees said to Jesus, "Hey, it's unlawful to harvest on a Sabbath, what are your disciples doing?" Jesus then went on to explain about a time when David went into the house of God to eat sacred bread meant only for the priests. He and his companions were hungry, so they fulfilled their need.

What this verse is telling us is not to take the Sabbath so literally that it causes harm, unhealthy sacrifice or deprivation. Don't use the Sabbath as a way to punish yourself, or others, or to support your tendencies to be a martyr. Remember, you left that one at the door.

God wants us to be taken care of. Just because it's a Sabbath day, or *your* chosen day of rest, doesn't mean that you still shouldn't take care of your needs. By all means, it's okay to fix a meal and eat! Just as it was not only okay, but far better, for David and his companions to eat sacred bread than go hungry and starve.

REFLECTION & PRAYER:

_____

_____

_____

_____

_____

_____

_____

_____

_____

_____

_____

_____

_____

_____

_____

_____

_____

_____

_____

_____

_____

_____

_____

_____

_____

_____

_____

Day 4

21 Six days you shall work, but on the seventh day you shall rest. In plowing time and in harvest you shall rest.

(Exodus 34:21 ESV)

No matter what season of life we're in, we need rest. Some seasons are more heavy loaded, and some seasons may seem light in comparison. Each season serves a purpose, and leads into the next (meaning, the next season depends on or is affected by the current season).

In times where life seems to be giving you more responsibilities or challenges than you seem to think you can handle, you might be apt to think "I don't have time to rest." My plea to you is that in every time when you think you don't have time, that is the exact time when you need to rest the most.

I know, it seems counterintuitive, but trust me. Plowing and harvest times are intense seasons for farmers. It's often long days and hard work, in contrast to growing seasons where it's more "maintenance and monitoring." Apologies to any farmers out there if I've botched or misrepresented your work in this example.

My point is simply this: if you don't take time to rest during the seasons of hard work, you will not be able to sustain yourself to finish your work. This is true for any career - from corporate C-Suite executives to the stay-at-home Moms. You can't just power through and wait for an "easier" season to rest. It doesn't work that way. Rest now, so you can make it to the next season.

REFLECTION & PRAYER:

_____

_____

_____

_____

_____

_____

_____

_____

_____

_____

_____

_____

_____

_____

_____

_____

_____

_____

_____

_____

_____

_____

_____

_____

Day 5

9 So then, there remains a Sabbath rest for the people of God, 10 for whoever has entered God's rest has also rested from his works as God did from his.

(Hebrews 4:9-10 ESV)

How beautiful it is that God gives us the same sweet rest that He himself took on the seventh day. The NLT version of verse 9 translates to a "special" rest. It is special. A special, Sabbath rest just for us. And when we enter into the special rest, we are likening ourselves to God, in His image.

God is mighty, He is love, He is grace, He is so many things - too many to list here. How wonderful, how beautiful, how special it is that we are given the invitation and the pure gift of resting like God rested.

REFLECTION & PRAYER:

_____

_____

_____

_____

_____

_____

_____

_____

_____

_____

_____

_____

_____

_____

_____

_____

_____

_____

_____

_____

_____

_____

_____

_____

LET GO AND LET GOD

Day 6

*28 **Come to me, all who labor and are heavy laden, and I will give you rest.** 29 **Take my yoke upon you, and learn from me, for I am gentle and lowly in heart, and you will find rest for your souls.** 30 **For my yoke is easy, and my burden is light.***

(Matthew 11:28-30 ESV)

If there is one verse in the entire Bible that defines my walk with Jesus, this is it. It's one of the first verses I memorized and it's the one I return to time and time again. No matter how many times I am reminded to give it all to God, I still need a reminder.

God's ways are lighter. His ways are gentle. His willingness to help us is unquestionable. We don't need to do it all ourselves, struggling through and grinding our teeth with dirt on our face and splinters under our fingernails. No, oh no. Our burdens, our stress, our overwhelm... God wants it all. He's asking for it.

The right way doesn't have to be the hard way. It's not the mindset of "if it's not hard it's not worth it." God's mindset is to let it be easy for us, and let Him carry the load.

REFLECTION & PRAYER:

_____

_____

_____

_____

_____

_____

_____

_____

_____

_____

_____

_____

_____

_____

_____

_____

_____

_____

_____

Day 7

22 Cast your burden on the Lord, and he will sustain you;
(Psalm 55:22a ESV)

I have this little silver stone engraved with the words "let go let God." I bought it for $1.00 at our local Christian bookstore, but it is worth so much more than what I paid for it. I keep it in my purse, where the coins are, so that every time I go in to make change or pay with a quarter I am reminded of what it means.

Every doubt, every fear, every negative thought becomes a burden for us and weighs us down if we don't release it. Imagine a backpack and inside is every negative thought - all the doubt, fear, guilt, shame, worry, anxiety, anger, resentment, etc. Imagine each one of those were stones, except they're not the little shiny silver stone I carry in my purse. These stones are big, round and rough. Imagine how heavy that backpack might become. My back hurts just thinking about it!

God doesn't want us to carry that weight - those burdens - on our own. He wants us to give them to Him, so He can carry us through whatever it is that we are going through.

Empty your backpack out. Give your stones to God.

REFLECTION & PRAYER:

_____

_____

_____

_____

_____

_____

_____

_____

_____

_____

_____

_____

_____

_____

_____

_____

_____

_____

_____

_____

_____

_____

_____

_____

_____

_____

FINDING SOLITUDE

Day 8

29 Jesus went on from there and walked beside the Sea of Galilee. And he went up on the mountain and sat down there.
(Matthew 15:29 ESV)

Often times when my mind is troubled or I've been working too hard, I find that a hike to the mid-top of a mountain or a stroll by the river is exactly what I need to clear my head. The view from above or the sound of the rushing water seem to make everything else melt away - even if just temporarily.

Does this ever happen to you? Do you ever feel like you just want to go outside? No particular reason, you just want to be in nature, smell the fresh air, feel the sun on your face, look up to the clouds. I know I'm not the only one!

I think Jesus knew what he was doing when he went out into nature. Being by the water and up on the mountain gave him time to be alone and reflect. It gave him time to be with his Heavenly Father. To pray. To be in solitude. To restore and rejuvenate himself so he could continue to heal the masses that were following him.

Jesus knew that time alone in nature was good for his mind and body. He knew it was good for his soul. It's good for you too.

Find time in your day to go out in nature, alone, and reflect.

REFLECTION & PRAYER:

_____

_____

_____

_____

_____

_____

_____

_____

_____

_____

_____

_____

_____

_____

_____

_____

Day 9

10 But [afterward], when His brothers had gone up to the feast, He went up too, not publicly [with a caravan], but quietly [because He did not want to be noticed].

(John 7:10 AMP)

"You go on ahead, I'll catch up." There could be several reasons Jesus didn't go to the feast with the caravan, but my guess is he just needed a moment (or several) to be alone.

You've been in a similar circumstance too I'm sure. People grasping for your time and attention, heaviness on your heart, swirling thoughts in your head that won't go away. Whatever the circumstance, I'm sure you've thought to yourself once or twice, "I just need a moment alone!"

It's okay to need quiet, to want quiet, to have quiet. Finding solitude amongst the crazy chaos of today's world is important.

You'll get to the party eventually, but maybe take the slower scenic route instead.

REFLECTION & PRAYER:

_____

_____

_____

_____

_____

_____

_____

_____

_____

_____

_____

_____

_____

_____

_____

_____

_____

_____

_____

_____

_____

_____

_____

_____

Day 10

32 *And they went to a place called Gethsemane. And he said to his disciples, "**Sit here while I pray.**"*

(Mark 14:32 ESV)

Jesus had spent the evening with his disciples, breaking bread, and preparing them for the events to follow - his betrayal, arrest and crucifixion. Jesus knew that his time was coming to an end, and now it was even more important for him to find a spot to pray.

He was entirely alone, a little ways up the path from his disciples. We learn this in verse 35 "After going a little farther..."

Jesus was troubled, distressed and overwhelmed. He didn't turn to his disciples for comfort. He turned to his Father, alone, in solitude.

How often do you seek comfort in others? How often do you seek comfort in spending time with God?

REFLECTION & PRAYER:

_____

_____

_____

_____

_____

_____

_____

_____

_____

_____

_____

_____

_____

_____

_____

_____

_____

_____

_____

_____

_____

_____

_____

_____

_____

_____

Day 11

35 Very early in the morning, while it was still dark, Jesus got up, left the house and went off to a solitary place, where he prayed.

(Mark 1:35 NIV)

In this busy world we live in it seems harder and harder to find time to enjoy a little peace and quiet. Getting up earlier is becoming one of the only solutions to carving out a little quiet time, although the competition is tough! A pre-dawn exercise class at the gym, an hour long commute to work, the bright-eyed toddler ready to play patty cake with your eye lids. There's always something that seems more important in the wee hours of the morning.

I'm not advocating that you get up at 3 o'clock in the morning just to pray, unless of course that fits in your lifestyle and you're in bed for the night at noon (okay, maybe that's a little exaggeration).

Here's the point, Jesus did what he had to do to find his peace and quiet time. He left the house. If you are too distracted to sit in solitude with God at home, by all means, go somewhere else (remember that nature thing earlier?).

Do what you have to do to... but be smart about it.

REFLECTION & PRAYER:

_____

_____

_____

_____

_____

_____

_____

_____

_____

_____

_____

_____

_____

_____

_____

_____

_____

_____

_____

_____

_____

_____

_____

_____

_____

_____

_____

_____

_____

Day 12

16 But Jesus often withdrew to lonely places and prayed.
(Luke 5:16 NIV)

Have you ever tried to have a serious, heart-felt conversation with someone on the phone while people right next to you are talking? Maybe they're in their own conversation, or maybe they're actually trying to talk to you. It's distracting, isn't it?

My kids have this superpower phone radar. Any time I'm about to get on the phone, they come running over and "need" me for something. I could spend fifteen minutes getting them set up with a snack, their homework or a tv show, explaining to them that they can't bother me. "Yeah, okay" they tell me. And then, without fail, the phone isn't even up to my ear yet and I can hear them coming...

What if that phone call was God calling?

No wonder Jesus went to be alone to pray. He didn't want distractions. He didn't want kids "needing" him - or whoever the superpower phone radar people are in your life.

Find your solitude so you can enjoy your time with God, without distractions, without interruptions, without excuses.

REFLECTION & PRAYER:

_____

_____

_____

_____

_____

_____

_____

_____

_____

_____

_____

_____

_____

_____

_____

_____

_____

_____

_____

_____

_____

_____

_____

_____

_____

_____

_____

FINDING STRENGTH

Day 13

7 *"Blessed is the man who trusts in the Lord, whose trust is the Lord. 8 He is like a tree planted by water, that sends out its roots by the stream, and does not fear when heat comes, for its leaves remain green, and is not anxious in the year of drought, for it does not cease to bear fruit."*

(Jeremiah 17:7-8 ESV)

This tree represents someone who trusts and finds strength in the Lord. The previous verse describes a shrub as someone who does not trust in the Lord, dwelling in a parched, uninhabited, salt land wilderness (verse 6). I don't know about you, but I would much rather be the tree.

Just like this tree can withstand all seasons because of the Lord, so can we withstand all seasons. If we set our roots in Jesus, and if we fully trust him, no matter what circumstance or season of life we're in, we know that God's got our back.

Setting our roots in Jesus doesn't just happen though. We have to consciously plant ourselves in the right spot, surrounded by the right people to support us. When we do that, it's like the roots of the tree drinking the water from the stream, always having enough to withstand any drought.

Think of your self-care time as the roots of the tree. Every time you are saying yes to yourself and spending time with God you are sending your roots out into the stream. Filling yourself up so when the drought comes (those curveballs that life always throws at you unexpectedly), you are prepared with enough water in your roots to last through the season.

Plant your tree, send your roots out into the stream, and find your strength in the Lord.

REFLECTION & PRAYER:

_____

_____

_____

_____

_____

_____

_____

_____

_____

_____

_____

Day 14

29 He gives power to the faint, and to him who has no might he increases strength. 30 Even youths shall faint and be weary, and young men shall fall exhausted; 31 but they who wait for the Lord shall renew their strength; they shall mount up with wings like eagles; they shall run and not be weary; they shall walk and not faint.

(Isaiah 40:29-31 ESV)

Even the strongest, most fit, in shape human beings will eventually fall down in exhaustion... without God. We can try to do it all on our own, and no matter how good we are, how much we've practiced, how much effort we put in, how long we take, eventually we will fail... without God.

We must learn to lean on God and turn to Him for renewal. God gives us strength!

In the oddest situations, when we know that on paper we should be so tired, but there is this unexplainable strength and renewed energy... it's God. It's puzzling at times, the strength people have to carry on, to keep going, to take one more step, but they do and they can.

Have you ever run a marathon? Or watched one? If I were to run a marathon - which is not likely *at all* - I know I would need to depend on God for my strength. Maybe running is a bad example. Let's take hot yoga. That, I have done. That, I have prayed my way through! Sweat dripping into my eyeballs and my body begging to tap out and call "Uncle" but then I pray, and God gives me strength to continue on.

Use God's strength when you have none left. Use it when your cup is empty and dry. Use it when you need strength to do something to fill your cup. He'll tell you it's okay, I promise.

REFLECTION & PRAYER:

_____

_____

_____

_____

_____

_____

_____

_____

_____

_____

_____

_____

_____

_____

_____

_____

_____

_____

_____

_____

_____

MARY AND MARTHA

Day 15

*38 Now as they went on their way, Jesus entered a village. And a woman named Martha welcomed him into her house. 39 And she had a sister called Mary, who sat at the Lord's feet and listened to his teaching. 40 But Martha was distracted with much serving. And she went up to him and said, "Lord, do you not care that my sister has left me to serve alone? Tell her then to help me." 41 But the Lord answered her, "**Martha, Martha, you are anxious and troubled about many things, 42 but one thing is necessary. Mary has chosen the good portion, which will not be taken away from her.**"*

(Luke 10:38-42 ESV)

Mary or Martha? Who are you most like?

I can recall several times when my husband would be sitting on the couch after dinner while I was in the kitchen cleaning up and doing dishes. Every time my thoughts go to "how come he's just sitting there?!" Now, before you get all upset and defensive let me just say that there are equal times when he's the one cleaning up and doing dishes after dinner.

So, while I'm wondering what he's thinking - *that he can just relax while I do all the work* - I have to say I know exactly what he's thinking. It's the same thing I think when I'm the one sitting on the couch and he's in the kitchen, "I'm tired, I've had a long day, I just need a moment to rest."

We may not be hanging out with Jesus in the living room, but we are honoring the need to rest and not be doing and busy all the time. It's important to recognize when you need those moments. It's important to give yourself permission to have them, with or without Jesus.

REFLECTION & PRAYER:

_____

_____

_____

_____

_____

_____

_____

_____

_____

_____

_____

_____

_____

_____

TAKING CARE

Day 16

3 Elijah was afraid and ran for his life. When he came to Beersheba in Judah, he left his servant there, 4 while he himself went a day's journey into the wilderness. He came to a broom bush, sat down under it and prayed that he might die. "I have had enough, Lord," he said. "Take my life; I am no better than my ancestors." 5 Then he lay down under the bush and fell asleep. All at once an angel touched him and said, "Get up and eat." 6 He looked around, and there by his head was some bread baked over hot coals, and a jar of water. He ate and drank and then lay down again. 7 The angel of the Lord came back a second time and touched him and said, "Get up and eat, for the journey is too much for you." 8 So he got up and ate and drank. Strengthened by that food, he traveled forty days and forty nights until he reached Horeb, the mountain of God. 9 There he went into a cave and spent the night.

(1 Kings 19:3-9 NIV)

Sometimes we have to simply get back to the basics. The basics of what we need to survive: food, water and sleep.

In this story Elijah felt depressed and lonely. Anyone else ever felt that? Anyone? Yeah, me too! Elijah was at a breaking point. He was ready to give up, in fact, that was his prayer. I've been there too.

God took care of Elijah and provided an angel with food and water. Elijah slept some more, and then the angel came back to give him more food, in order to sustain him for the journey. He made it to where he was going and then guess what he did again? He slept.

Sometimes our bodies are so tired, our minds are so overworked, or our emotions have been strung out for so long that we simply just need the basics. Food, water and sleep.

REFLECTION & PRAYER:

_____

_____

_____

_____

_____

_____

_____

_____

_____

_____

_____

_____

Day 17

19 Or do you not know that your body is a temple of the Holy Spirit within you, whom you have from God? You are not your own, 20 for you were bought with a price. So glorify God in your body.

(1 Corinthians 6:19-20 ESV)

We are merely temporary bodies in these holy vessels that God has given us. We could treat them as temporary and trash them - um, probably not a good idea - or we could treat them as the holy gift they are with respect and care. Yes, let's do that!

Think of your body as a delicate crystal vase. What happens if the crystal vase cracks and breaks? It becomes useless. Or even more appropriate, think of your body as holy and sacred bronze or silver or gold. What happens if those metals are left out in the elements to weather and tarnish? They don't shine like they used to.

Be good to your body. Nourish it, care for it, give it time to recover and heal. Your body is a magnificent miracle and you can push it further than you probably believe is possible, but that doesn't mean you have to or should. Treat your body like the holy vessel it is.

REFLECTION & PRAYER:

_____

_____

_____

_____

_____

_____

_____

_____

_____

_____

_____

_____

_____

_____

_____

_____

_____

_____

_____

_____

_____

_____

_____

_____

_____

_____

Day 18

2 It is in vain that you rise up early and go late to rest, eating the bread of anxious toil; for he gives to his beloved sleep.

(Psalm 127:2 ESV)

I'm not a morning person, and I'm not a night owl. That makes me an I-like-my-sleep person. I'm thinking of starting a club. You can join if you want! The only requirements are that you promise to (try to) get 7-9 hours of sleep each night. Not each week, not every so often or occasionally, but all the time!

Now, I know that sometimes we have babies who need feeding in the night or toddlers (or ten year olds) who need a little hug after a bad dream. I understand that sometimes there are legitimate reasons why 7-9 hours isn't possible.

Here's the deal though, those instances have to be the rare occasion.

I won't lie to you. I've had my share of late nights working (or binge watching tv - don't judge), but I don't make it a habit. I know when those times are coming so I can prepare myself and my family. I allow for recovery time and I know that when I'm extra tired I'm not going to be at my best.

Don't you want to be at your best? Don't you want to be God's best? You already are, by the way, but making sure you get enough sleep allows you to feel the best.

Sweet dreams…

REFLECTION & PRAYER:

ASKING FOR HELP

Day 19

13 *The next day Moses took his seat to serve as judge for the people, and they stood around him from morning till evening.* 14 *When his father-in-law saw all that Moses was doing for the people, he said, "What is this you are doing for the people? Why do you alone sit as judge, while all these people stand around you from morning till evening?"* 15 *Moses answered him, "Because the people come to me to seek God's will.* 16 *Whenever they have a dispute, it is brought to me, and I decide between the parties and inform them of God's decrees and instructions."* 17 *Moses' father-in-law replied, "What you are doing is not good.* 18 *You and these people who come to you will only wear yourselves out. The work is too heavy for you; you cannot handle it alone.* 19 *Listen now to me and I will give you some advice, and may God be with you. You must be the people's representative before God and bring their disputes to him.* 20 *Teach them his decrees and instructions, and show them the way they are to live and how they are to behave.* 21 *But select capable men from all the people—men who fear God, trustworthy men who hate dishonest gain—and appoint them as officials over thousands, hundreds, fifties and tens.* 22 *Have them*

serve as judges for the people at all times, but have them bring every difficult case to you; the simple cases they can decide themselves. That will make your load lighter, because they will share it with you. 23 If you do this and God so commands, you will be able to stand the strain, and all these people will go home satisfied." 24 Moses listened to his father-in-law and did everything he said. 25 He chose capable men from all Israel and made them leaders of the people, officials over thousands, hundreds, fifties and tens. 26 They served as judges for the people at all times. The difficult cases they brought to Moses, but the simple ones they decided themselves. 27 Then Moses sent his father-in-law on his way, and Jethro returned to his own country.

(Exodus 18:13-27 NIV)

This is a big one. Asking for help. I wonder, if you had the same subconscious suggestion growing up that I did. Asking for help meant I was weak or incapable. I don't necessarily know where I learned that from. No one ever literally told me that. It was just a thought pattern that I came to believe as true, and then I had to break it.

If you believe that asking for help means you're weak or incapable let me just stop right now for a minute to tell you otherwise. There is nothing wrong with needing an extra helping hand - for whatever reason - and asking for it.

When you were a baby did you come out walking? No! You had to learn to walk, and I know you fell down along the way. You've landed on your knees, fallen on your behind, maybe even pancaked on your face. Point is, you fell, and likely someone was there to help you back up. They didn't judge you or get mad at you. They didn't call you weak and incapable. You didn't even have to ask for the help most of the time, they were just there.

What about when you learned to ride a bike? Was there someone there holding the seat, running alongside you, helping you balance until you could do it on your own?

Or maybe when you couldn't reach a glass in the upper cabinet. Did you ask for help?

When did we decide that asking for help was a bad thing? When did we decide that needing help made us weak and incapable?

One of the bravest, most courageous things a person could ever do is to ask for help when they really, really need it. I'm talking about help in terms of someone to watch the kids so you can get out of the house by yourself before you literally go crazy and climb the walls. I'm talking about asking for help with household chores and responsibilities so you can breathe for five minutes and possibly even get to bed on time (remember that sleep thing?). I'm talking about asking for help with addiction, because let's face it, that is real. I'm talking about asking for help with deadlines and projects and all the little tasks that get piled on your desk at work, glaring at you while you're silently drowning inside, saying "I've got this" on the outside.

It's okay if you don't "got this"!

Ask for help when you need it. Don't wait until it's so overwhelming you don't even know where to start digging out of the pit you're in. Ask for help even if you don't know how someone could help you. You'll figure it out and find a way. Ask God... He'll gladly show you.

In this passage Moses was doing it all. He was the judge of all the people and he worked tirelessly from morning until evening taking care of all their needs. In today's society that's called burning the candle at both ends. Poor Moses was probably exhausted!

Thankfully, his father-in-law knew how to come in and help Moses learn to delegate. He knew that what Moses was doing was not sustainable and eventually he would wear himself out. What an incredible lesson in asking for help!

You do not have to do everything on your own. You do not have to save the day and be the hero who did it all. You do not have to compromise your strength and talents when you ask for help. In fact, you will become even stronger when you let others help you.

Practice asking for help. In today's reflection and prayer, ask God to show you where you could ask someone for help. Be bold, be courageous, be brave and go ask.

REFLECTION & PRAYER:

_____

_____

_____

_____

_____

_____

_____

WHO AM I ASKING FOR HELP? WHAT AM I ASKING?:

_____

_____

_____

_____

_____

_____

_____

_____

_____

_____

_____

_____

_____

_____

_____

_____

_____

_____

_____

_____

_____

_____

_____

_____

_____

_____

_____

FINDING REST

Day 20

1 The Lord is my shepherd; I shall not want. 2 He makes me lie down in green pastures. He leads me beside still waters. 3 He restores my soul. He leads me in paths of righteousness for his name's sake.

(Psalms 23:1-3 ESV)

Yesterday was a big day. Well done on getting through it. I hope it opened some doors for you, or at least some conversations. Today, we get to talk about rest. Ahhhh, yes, take a nice deep breath as you settle in.

I love this verse! Thinking about the imagery of the green pasture and the still waters, and I can't help but feel a sense of calm and peace.

God knows where to lead us so we can be renewed and restored. He knows when we need rest, when to simply stop. He does all of this so that we can be filled up. We have to listen.

It's in these quiet times of rest and stillness that God speaks to us. He's always with us, but we can't hear Him and know what He's trying to tell us unless we stop.

I know sometimes it's hard to slow down, let alone stop entirely, but we have to. We weren't designed to be the energizer bunny. God designed us to have times of rest. Let's honor that, knowing that when we do stop to rest, God will mightily fill us up.

REFLECTION & PRAYER:

_____

_____

_____

_____

_____

_____

_____

_____

_____

_____

_____

_____

_____

_____

_____

_____

_____

_____

Day 21

14 And he said, "My presence will go with you, and I will give you rest."

(Exodus 33:14 ESV)

When God commanded Moses to go, to leave Mount Sinai, Moses was a little bit anxious. I'm speculating here, it doesn't actually say that, but I think it's fair to assume his nerves were a bit high. Remember, Moses wasn't the most self-confident in his abilities to lead or speak to the people in the beginning.

Moses was questioning who God would send with him. He knew that God found favor in him, we see this in verses 12. I believe Moses was ready for more. He was ready to know God more. He even says in verse 13, "please show me now your ways,"

How awesome is it that God Himself told Moses He would go with him. God's presence would always be with Moses. God's presence is always with us as well. If that isn't comforting I don't know what is.

God is always with us. He rests in our hearts and in our bodies through the Holy Spirit. As God rests within us, He also provides rest for us. We merely have to turn to Him, to tap into the Holy Spirit within us, and ask for Him to provide rest.

REFLECTION & PRAYER:

_____

_____

_____

_____

_____

_____

_____

_____

_____

_____

_____

_____

_____

_____

_____

_____

_____

_____

_____

_____

_____

_____

_____

_____

_____

_____

_____

_____

Day 22

25 For I will satisfy the weary soul, and every languishing soul I will replenish."

(Jeremiah 31:25 ESV)

The dictionary defines weary as: "physically or mentally exhausted by hard work, exertion, strain, etc.; fatigued; tired." Does this ever sound like you?

What would it look like or feel like to know that no matter how weary you are, God can fill you back up. He can satisfy your emptiness. And not just your soul, but *every* soul.

God is mighty. He is like a faucet of running water. Always on, always there to fill our cups (ourselves), to give us back what we have spent.

Yes, God, fill me back up!

REFLECTION & PRAYER:

_____

_____

_____

_____

_____

_____

_____

_____

_____

_____

_____

_____

_____

_____

_____

_____

_____

_____

_____

_____

_____

_____

_____

_____

_____

_____

_____

_____

_____

_____

Day 23

24 If you lie down, you will not be afraid; when you lie down, your sleep will be sweet.

(Proverbs 3:24 ESV)

Isn't it the worst when you are crazy tired, you finally get to bed, and instead of falling right to sleep and drifting off to dreamland you're staring at the ceiling, wide awake, thinking about all the gazillion things you need to do tomorrow, didn't do today, or forgot about yesterday?

Maybe it's not so much the anxiety of the stock ticker to do list running in your head, it's bigger worries, like how you're going to pay the mortgage, or the medical bills.

Or maybe it's the first night alone after you've lost a loved one or your home.

There are countless reasons why you can't seem to fall asleep. You're not alone.

God is with you, always. Turn your focus on Him. Let Him be your pillow to rest your head upon. If you don't know why you're not sleeping, ask Him. He knows what's on your heart and in your mind. He also knows you need your sleep.

Restless, broken sleep won't do. That's not good enough for you. That's not good enough for God. Sweet sleep is what God will bring you.

Once again…. Sweet dreams.

REFLECTION & PRAYER:

_____

_____

_____

_____

_____

_____

_____

_____

_____

_____

_____

_____

_____

_____

_____

_____

_____

_____

_____

_____

_____

_____

_____

_____

_____

Day 24

5 I lay down and slept; I woke again, for the Lord sustained me.
(Psalm 3:5 ESV)

When our first son was born my husband held him all night long. He slept in his arms the entire night. That was the only time he slept through the night until we brought his little brother home from the hospital two years and nine months later. I'm not kidding!

After that it was another year plus of getting up in the night to feed and change and do all the baby stuff again. Add that all up and it was literally fours years before I myself slept through the night again. And as a mom, with mom ears (in other words, I hear everything), my sleep-through-anything days are over.

You may ask or wonder, first, how come we didn't so something about the sleeping issues earlier? Trust me, we tried everything. I've got the documentation to prove it!

Second, you might ask or wonder, how did I survive on that much lack of sleep? That is an excellent question! It was by the grace of God, who ironically enough, I did not have a relationship with yet.

Why did I share all this with you? Because God will sustain you, wake you, energize you, recharge you, in ways you may never comprehend. You don't have to understand it all. You just have to know that God will allow you to sleep. He will wake you when it's time. So go ahead, sleep hard, and God will see you in the morning.

REFLECTION & PRAYER:

THE EXAMPLE

Day 25

*30 The apostles returned to Jesus and told him all that they had done and taught. 31 And he said to them, "**Come away by yourselves to a desolate place and rest a while.**" For many were coming and going, and they had no leisure even to eat. 32 And they went away in the boat to a desolate place by themselves.*

(Mark 6:30-32 ESV)

The best way we can get to know God is to get to know Jesus. The best way to get to know Jesus is to follow his lead and his example. He was the greatest example of how to love - not just others, but himself.

Jesus realized that when work was being done, when his disciples were teaching as he had directed them to, energy was being outputted. The only way to regain that energy was to rest. So Jesus basically told them, "Hey, you guys need a break, let's find some solitude."

The disciples had been working so hard, they were so busy, they didn't even have time to eat. Sound familiar? Ever work through lunch? Was it intentional? Even if it wasn't, you should not let that become a habit.

Take the lead from Jesus and follow his example. Give yourself a break. Find solitude. Rest. And don't forget to eat.

REFLECTION & PRAYER:

_____

_____

_____

_____

_____

_____

_____

_____

_____

_____

_____

_____

_____

_____

_____

Day 26

12 While Jesus was in one of the towns, a man came along who was covered with leprosy. When he saw Jesus, he fell with his face to the ground and begged him, "Lord, if you are willing, you can make me clean." 13 Jesus reached out his hand and touched the man. **"I am willing,"** *he said.* **"Be clean!"** *And immediately the leprosy left him. 14 Then Jesus ordered him,* **"Don't tell anyone, but go, show yourself to the priest and offer the sacrifices that Moses commanded for your cleansing, as a testimony to them."** *15 Yet the news about him spread all the more, so that crowds of people came to hear him and to be healed of their sicknesses. 16 But Jesus often withdrew to lonely places and prayed.*

(Luke 5:12-16 NIV)

Jesus was many things: compassionate, humble, faithful. One trait that I am bringing to your attention again is his solitude. Jesus had just healed a man with leprosy, which caused crowds of people to come for their own healing.

What's interesting to note in this passage is that we don't see Jesus staying up all night to heal every last one. Quite the opposite, we see Jesus going off by himself to pray. He knew his priorities. He valued doing his own self-care. He knew that he couldn't heal them all without first pouring back into himself.

REFLECTION & PRAYER:

_____

_____

_____

_____

_____

_____

_____

_____

_____

_____

_____

_____

_____

_____

_____

_____

_____

_____

_____

_____

_____

_____

_____

_____

_____

_____

_____

_____

Day 27

*35 On that day, when evening had come, he said to them, "**Let us go across to the other side.**" 36 And leaving the crowd, they took him with them in the boat, just as he was. And other boats were with him. 37 And a great windstorm arose, and the waves were breaking into the boat, so that the boat was already filling. 38 But he was in the stern, asleep on the cushion. And they woke him and said to him, "Teacher, do you not care that we are perishing?" 39 And he awoke and rebuked the wind and said to the sea, "**Peace! Be still!**" And the wind ceased, and there was a great calm. 40 He said to them, "**Why are you so afraid? Have you still no faith?**"*

(Mark 4:35-40 ESV)

Jesus liked to get away from the crowds. It wasn't because he was uncomfortable amongst people. He wasn't an introvert (again, personal speculation here). Jesus liked to get away from the crowds because he knew that's when he could find rest, be with his Father, pray, or simply sleep.

That was the case in the boat. Jesus had laid down to rest and sleep (he knew he needed to, he wanted to, he didn't feel guilty for doing so), and was fast asleep until his disciples woke him in fear for the storm they were in.

We could take several angles on this passage, but the one I want to point out is that Jesus was not afraid to sleep. He wasn't concerned with continuing to serve. He had already taught through parables that day. He had fulfilled his work for the day.

The storm could be metaphorical as well, showing us that no matter what crazy chaos is happening in the world around us, if Jesus can take time to sleep, then so can we.

Jesus had faith, not only in his ability to calm the storm, but in his decision to lay down for rest and sleep. He put himself first, not to be selfish, but because he knew he had to.

Be like Jesus, lay down for rest and sleep.

REFLECTION & PRAYER:

_____

_____

_____

_____

_____

_____

_____

_____

_____

_____

_____

_____

_____

_____

_____

_____

_____

_____

Day 28

13 Now when Jesus heard this, he withdrew from there in a boat to a desolate place by himself. But when the crowds heard it, they followed him on foot from the towns. 14 When he went ashore he saw a great crowd, and he had compassion on them and healed their sick. 15 Now when it was evening, the disciples came to him and said, "This is a desolate place, and the day is now over; send the crowds away to go into the villages and buy food for themselves." 16 But Jesus said, "They need not go away; you give them something to eat."

(...Jesus proceeds to feed the five thousand with two fish and five loaves of bread...)

22 Immediately he made the disciples get into the boat and go before him to the other side, while he dismissed the crowds. 23 And after he had dismissed the crowds, he went up on the mountain by himself to pray. When evening came, he was there alone,

(Matthew 14:13-16, 22-23 ESV)

Again, we see Jesus withdrawing from the crowds. And again, we see them following him. I mean, wouldn't you? This time, however, Jesus pulls out a little miracle and feeds a few people. Well, five thousand people!

What's important to note here is that Jesus performed this miracle after he heard the news of the be-heading of John the Baptist. That's why Jesus had left in a boat, to go mourn and grieve. He was sidetracked when the crowds followed him.

There are two messages here as we look at Jesus for the example. One, he consistently retreats to find solitude. Two, he had to adjust his plans and become flexible.

Jesus desperately wanted to be by himself to mourn the death of his friend and brother. As we know, compassion took over and he stayed to heal the crowds and then subsequently feed them. But, as soon as he was done he didn't say, "oh well, I didn't have time to mourn today, maybe it wasn't meant to be." No! As soon as he was done he immediately sent his disciples off to go ahead, and he himself went up on the mountain to pray.

Jesus still prioritized his solitude. It just didn't happen the way he thought or in the timing he was anticipating.

REFLECTION & PRAYER:

_____

_____

_____

_____

_____

_____

_____

_____

_____

_____

_____

_____

_____

_____

GOD'S TIMING

Day 29

7 Be still before the Lord and wait patiently for him; fret not yourself over the one who prospers in his way, over the man who carries out evil devices!

(Psalm 37:7 ESV)

Have you ever prayed for patience? Yeah, it never really works out that well does it? God seems to always give you a circumstance or situation to work through to force you to need more patience. Thanks, God!

Do you ever find yourself comparing yourself to others? Okay, maybe that's a rhetorical question. I'd like to meet the person who never compares. Oh wait, that was Jesus.

Other people will get to where you're heading before you. Don't worry about it. Like I tell my boys, "Focus on yourself." You don't know how they got there, you don't know their story, you don't know if they'll be able to sustain it.

If you do what *you* need to do, taking care of *yourself*, finding solitude and rest, leaning on God for strength, then it doesn't matter how long it will take you because you will be well-equipped and fully prepared for the journey.

REFLECTION & PRAYER:

_____

_____

_____

_____

_____

_____

_____

_____

_____

_____

_____

_____

_____

_____

_____

_____

_____

_____

_____

_____

_____

Day 30

21 Martha said to Jesus, "Lord, if you had been here, my brother would not have died.
32 Now when Mary came to where Jesus was and saw him, she fell at his feet, saying to him, "Lord, if you had been here, my brother would not have died."

(John 11:21, 32 ESV)

Remember Mary and Martha? Well, in this passage we are looking at how they both got upset with Jesus because he took too long to get to them and save Lazarus from dying. We know what happens, it's like watching a movie when you know what's on the other side of the door but the character in the movie has no clue.

Jesus raises Lazarus from the dead. It's another miracle. It's another lesson in patience and God's timing.

Sometimes we are so anxious to get to where we're going, or to accomplish our task and reach our goals, that we fail to acknowledge the greater power. We fail to believe. We fail to have faith.

God wants to be a part of our lives all the time. Daily, and throughout the day, not just in the emergencies. He doesn't want us to figure everything out on our own. He doesn't want us to forget that He can perform miracles.

Do you think that if Mary and Martha had trusted Jesus and put more faith in him they still would have been so upset at his timing? We can't really say because that's not how the story went. But if we pretend that was the case, do you think maybe they would have prevented some extra stress and worry?

Do you think there is a place in your life where you need to give up control of your timing, and have faith that God will work it out the way it's meant to be? Do you think if you let go, you would also release some stress and worry? What could that do for you?

God's timing is never our timing, but it is always perfect timing.

REFLECTION & PRAYER:

_____

_____

_____

_____

_____

_____

_____

_____

_____

_____

_____

_____

_____

_____

_____

_____

Day 31

10 "Be still, and know that I am God. I will be exalted among the nations, I will be exalted in the earth!"

(Psalm 46:10 ESV)

There is nothing that God cannot do. No amount of stress or anxiety will shake God. He can handle it all. All of it.

We start to get into trouble when we think we can handle it all, when we can handle it better. We take back control from God - or at least we attempt to - until we realize that was a bad idea.

It's like driving your car into a muddy rut in the middle of a dirt road. Your tire gets stuck. What's your first instinct? To gun it. Slam on the gas pedal in hopes that the tire will get un-stuck. But what happens instead? The tire just spins and spins and gets deeper and deeper into the mud.

We do the same thing with God. We try to take care of it all ourselves, until we're so far stuck in the mud we have no other option. That's when we cry out to God for help and rescue.

What if, instead of ignoring Him until we're out of options, we reached out to Him when the car starts slowing down, before we even get stuck in the mud to begin with? Or what if, when we do get stuck, instead of hitting the gas pedal, we stop, put the car in park and get out? Get out of God's way. Let Him call AAA and the fancy yellow tow truck.

Here's an even better option. What if, instead of trying to take the short cut down the muddy dirt road, we took a moment to listen to God? What are the directions He is giving us? Which road is He laying out for us?

None of us want to head down the dead-end or the impassible dirt road, but we do. What if we trusted God, knowing that there is nothing He cannot do, and let Him set the route and the itinerary?

REFLECTION & PRAYER:

_____

_____

_____

_____

_____

_____

_____

_____

_____

_____

_____

_____

_____

_____

_____

_____

_____

PAMELA ZIMMER

WHAT'S NEXT

Congratulations! You made it. We made it! I am so proud of you. I hope you're proud of you too. I bet you're wondering, what's next? While I can't tell you what the next thirty days will hold for you, I can encourage you to keep up with the habit you just created for yourself.

Keep practicing your self-care. Keep making time to find solitude, to find rest, to find strength. Keep making time for God.

Remind yourself about all the themes you explored over the last month. Each one was important, just like each area of your life and each part of your self-care routine is important. Use Jesus as the example - he was a great one!

I know that life will happen - it always does. Something will come up, someone will need you, somehow you'll forget how great you're feeling right now and this time you've prioritized for yourself won't be such a priority anymore. I know it will happen.

Here's what you do when it does: don't judge yourself, acknowledge that it's happening, and get back up on the horse. Start small again. Start with day one. Start over at the beginning, just start.

Ask for help. That was a big day when Moses learned to delegate. Do you think you can do that too? You don't have to do everything on your own. Don't be the martyr or the hero.

Life is full of unexpected twists and turns, potholes and speed bumps, dead-ends and muddy dirt roads. We are never going to avoid all the hazards, but we can be prepared for them. Staying in the Word, opening up your Bible, praying to God and loving yourself like Jesus... that's how you prepare yourself.

Put your oxygen mask on first. Listen to those airlines!

Fill up your cup. You can't pour when it's empty!

Sleep when you're tired, rest often and love yourself always.

Remember, self-care isn't selfish, it's essential. The Bible says so, and even Jesus took time to rest.

REFLECTION & PRAYER

"Prayer doesn't just change things - it changes
us. If we are diligent in seeking God, slowly
and surely we become better people."
-Joyce Meyer

On the following pages I've given you some extra room to
capture your thoughts and continue your reflection and
prayer. Use this space as you pray, asking God to show you
what is next for you.

REFLECTION & PRAYER:

_____

_____

_____

_____

_____

_____

_____

_____

_____

_____

_____

_____

REFLECTION & PRAYER:

REFLECTION & PRAYER:

REFLECTION & PRAYER:

_____

_____

_____

_____

_____

_____

_____

_____

_____

_____

_____

_____

_____

_____

_____

_____

_____

_____

_____

_____

_____

_____

_____

_____

REFLECTION & PRAYER:

_____

_____

_____

_____

_____

_____

_____

_____

_____

_____

_____

_____

_____

_____

_____

_____

_____

_____

_____

_____

_____

_____

_____

_____

REFLECTION & PRAYER:

REFLECTION & PRAYER:

CONNECT WITH PAMELA

To connect with Pamela and continue the self-care conversation you can find her online. She invites you to stay close, receive her support, and share your self-care journey with her.

Email: Pamela@PamelaZimmer.com

Website: www.PamelaZimmer.com

Facebook Business: Pamela Zimmer - Author, Speaker, Mentor
    https://www.facebook.com/SelfCareQueen/

Facebook Personal: Pamela Zimmer
    https://www.facebook.com/pamela.zimmer1

FREE Facebook Group: Self Care Isn't Selfish
    https://www.facebook.com/groups/selfcareisntselfish/

LinkedIn: Pamela (Sommer) Zimmer
    https://www.linkedin.com/in/pamelazimmer1/

Download Pamela's FREE GIFT "7 Simple Self-Care Secrets"
    http://pamelazimmer.com/selfcaresecrets
            OR
Text "selfcare1" to 444999

To inquire about having Pamela come speak to your group, send an email to Speaking@PamelaZimmer.com